LISTENING TO THE GROANS

LISTENING TO THE GROANS

A SPIRITUALITY *for* MINISTRY *and* MISSION

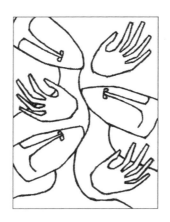

Trevor Hudson with Stephen Bryant

Illustrations by Jan L. Richardson

UPPER
ROOM BOOKS®
Nashville

LISTENING TO THE GROANS: A SPIRITUALITY FOR MINISTRY
AND MISSION
Text © 2007 by Trevor Hudson and Stephen D. Bryant
Art © 2007 by Jan L. Richardson
All rights reserved.

All Scripture quotations are from the New Revised Standard
Version Bible, copyright 1989, Division of Christian Education of
the National Council of the Churches of Christ in the United States
of America. Used by permission. All rights reserved.

Retreat adapted from a model written by Eileen Campbell-Reed,
which first appeared in *The Way of Transforming Discipleship*.

Cover design: LeftCoast Design
Cover and interior art: Jan L. Richardson
First Printing: 2007
ISBN: 978-0-8358-9933-8
PRINTED IN THE UNITED STATES OF AMERICA

WITH GRATITUDE

TO TOM WRIGHT, FOR WARMING MY
HEART AGAIN WITH THE BIBLICAL STORY

AND

TO DEBBIE, FOR HER LISTENING PRESENCE
AND COMPANIONSHIP IN MY LIFE

Contents

Introduction

A Spirituality for Ministry and Mission

I became a Christ–follower at the age of seventeen. The gracious invitation to "follow me," rooted in a great love that had sought me from my very beginnings, burned its way into my heart and evoked both desire and response. Ever since that moment of new beginning I have been learning from Jesus how to live the one life that I have been given. This search has connected me with the lives of many other seeking pilgrims along the Way. In recent years I have come to recognize this common seeking as a widespread yearning in the hearts of men and women for an authentic spirituality.

Spirituality is a slippery word. Some are suspicious of the term. For those whose daily lives revolve around frantic timetables of preparing breakfast, getting children to school on time, holding down a stressful eight–to–five job, paying monthly bills, and cleaning the house, spirituality sounds strange and impractical. It suggests another world of inactivity, passivity, and uninterrupted silences.

For those whose life experiences have been scarred by suffering and oppression, the term often suggests escapism, indifference, and uninvolvement. Indeed, spirituality needs definition. Spirituality is being intentional about the development of those convictions, attitudes, and actions through which the Christ–following life is shaped and given personal expression within our everyday lives.

Amidst this widespread yearning for a vital and real spirituality we need to be discerning. We need to be willing to listen to the groans in our world and within ourselves. Within contemporary Christian congregations some expressions of spirituality are foreign to the biblical tradition and unrelated to the spirit of the crucified and risen Lord. Some congregations are obsessively concerned with their own personal needs and have minimal concern for those who suffer and thus do not even enter the struggle for change in the world. Some others frequently endorse a spirituality of social struggle and involvement that avoids the biblical imperative for personal conversion and transformation. Such endorsement falls victim to the dangerous illusion, alive and well in our midst, that we can build a more equitable, compassionate, and just society while we remain the same and continue life as usual.

Wherever you may find yourself along the Way, may you discover in these words some nourishing food for the journey. It is my hope that in offering these few reflections on listening to the groans, all of us may become more radically open to the transformation that God is able to bring about in our personal and social lives. An authentic Christian spirituality always stretches toward the transforming of our personal lives and of the societies in which we live, work, and play. I will be immeasurably grateful if, in the lives of some fellow pilgrims and seekers, these reflections contribute to such a transformation.

–Trevor Hudson

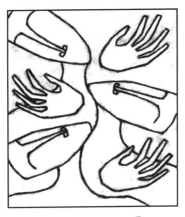

Listening to the Groans

A delightful story is told about the great scientist Dr. Albert Einstein, who was once allegedly on a train out of New York City. As the conductor was making his rounds, Einstein began to look through his pockets for his ticket. He couldn't find it. By the time the conductor arrived at Einstein's seat, he had emptied all his pockets, searched through his briefcase, and was proceeding on all fours to look around on the floor of the coach. When the conductor recognized Einstein, he said, "Don't worry about finding the ticket, Dr. Einstein. I trust you." In response, Einstein turned his head upward from his position on the floor and said, "Young man, this is not about trust. I need to find that ticket; otherwise I have no idea where I am going."

This story provides us with a helpful parable. All of us, as individual Christ-followers and as congregations, are riding the train of life. In order to arrive at our destination, the one that God has in mind for us, we need to have our ticket. If we don't, like Einstein, we may not know where we are heading. We may even get off at the wrong station. I want to describe this ticket in one simple phrase: listening to the groans. It is the ticket for all Christian ministry and mission. It is the ticket to evangelism, healing, pastoral care, community building, peace-making and so much more. As we listen to the groans of others, we build a bridge between our inner journey and the outer journey of those around us. In doing so, we find ourselves being delivered from a private spirituality. As we listen to the groans we find ourselves able to love God with all our hearts, souls, minds, and strength and to love our neighbors as ourselves.

Sadly, we who call ourselves by the name of Christ are not good at listening. During World War II theologian Dietrich Bonhoeffer was one of the few German Christians who resisted the tyranny of Hitler. In the midst of that national trauma, he helped build a confessing church. As a young adult I feasted on his books *The Cost of Discipleship* and *Letters and Papers from Prison.* Those books were manna for me in a time when I was trying to be faithful in the painful context that was then apartheid South Africa. In another book called *Life Together,* written over sixty years ago, Bonhoeffer wrote these words: "Many people are looking for an ear that will listen. They do not find it among Christians, because these Christians are talking where they should be listening."[1] He goes on to say that Christians who have stopped listening to their neighbor will soon stop listening to God as well.

In order to explore this ticket more deeply, I want us to explore Paul's words to the Romans in chapter 8, verses 22–27. These verses come midway between two popular biblical passages. At the beginning of the eighth chapter there is the wonderful text, a favorite of evangelicals, declaring that there is no condemnation for those who are in Christ Jesus (v. 1). At the end of the chapter there is the magnificent statement, a favorite of universalists, that neither death nor life, nor anything else in all creation will ever be able to separate us from the love of God that is in Christ Jesus our Lord. We are going to explore the scripture in between these two passages. In verses 22 through 27, we read about three groans to which all followers of Jesus need to listen. There is no shortcut from the first part of the chapter to the last part. The passage about the groans cannot be bypassed. Rather, as New Testament scholar Tom Wright has pointed out, verses 22–27 are the means by which these two grand statements are rooted in historical and theological reality.[2]

The passage tells us that three voices are groaning at the same time. They groan all around us, as well as within us. If we listen deeply, we can hear each one. These voices together help us to find our way towards God's destination for our lives and our world. As we listen to these groans we are led to a deeper faithfulness, both in our personal discipleship and in our life together as God's people. When we listen to the groans, we begin to have a much clearer understanding of how we can participate in God's wonderful dream for the mending of our broken world.

CREATION GROANS

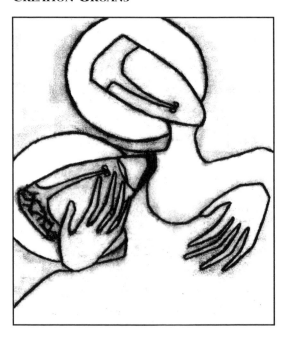

First of all, we need to listen to the groans of creation. In verse 22 Paul writes, "We know that the whole creation has been groaning in labor pains until now." This verse makes it clear that God is passionately concerned about the whole world. Our hearts and minds need to be deeply grasped by this reality. Too often we turn our backs on the world that God has made and loves. I remember being taught songs soon after my conversion as a teenager that encouraged me to view the world as separate from the saving work of Christ. I sang, "The world behind me, the cross before me ..."[5] Yet, the cross is in the world. Christ gets crucified in the world, before our eyes and our ears, every day of our lives. Did he not say, "Just as you did it to one of the least of these who are members of my family, you did it to me" (Matt. 25:40)?

Another song I sang went like this: "Turn your eyes upon Jesus, look full in his wonderful face, and the things of earth will grow strangely dim in the light of his glory and grace."[4] Although I can understand what the songwriter meant by this, I have found that the things of the world grow strangely clear in the light of Jesus Christ. Surely, since Jesus Christ is the light of the world, we can see its beauty and pain even more clearly and hear its laughter and cries more deeply. When we open our lives to Jesus, we are drawn more deeply into the world that he loved so much and for which he died.

Songs like these can often betray God's fierce love for the whole world. "For God so loved the world that he gave his only Son. . . . " Paul knew this, and so his concerns were always cosmic in scope. He knew that God's loving arms wrap around the globe and embrace every human being, whether they be Christian or Muslim or Buddhist or Jew or atheist; they

embrace every nation and culture and eth-
nicity; they embrace every aspect of what
it means to be human–the worlds of art
and music and finance and economics and
education and medicine and politics and
sport. God's arms embrace the trees and
mountains and forests and rivers and every
other living thing. God wants to put the
whole world right. As Hans Küng has written, "God's kingdom is creation healed."[5]

Verse 22 also says that this good creation
that God loves so much groans as in the
pains of childbirth. Paul goes beyond the
secular and simplistic ways in which our
world is so often described. For Paul the
world is not just neatly divided up into
good and bad, rich and poor, oppressed
and oppressor, saved and unsaved, east
and west. Rather, for Paul the condition of
the world can best be described with a
striking image–the image of a woman

groaning in labor. This is what the world is like. It is groaning in the pangs of giving birth to that new creation which God intends. It is groaning for its healing and its mending, so that in the end all tears may be dried and the world may be filled with laughter and joy and justice.

Now, if you and I are going to participate in God's great purposes of putting this world right, we will need to have our ticket. We dare not continue to preach or teach until we have heard the groans. The violence of the wars that we have experienced this past century have a way of making a mockery of words. After Auschwitz, Hiroshima, Vietnam, Cambodia, Rwanda, Iraq, all our words–especially about the healing and reconciliation of our world–sound hollow and cheap and glib. What does one really say after one reads that, since 1998, over four million people have lost their lives in the war in the Congo? As writer Richard Lischer says, we come to "the end of words."[6] However, it is often when we come to the end of words that true ministry begins. This is the moment when we begin to listen to the groans.

Sometimes, we will need to listen very carefully. The groans of those who suffer deeply can often be disguised. I became aware of this only recently. Together with my son I had gone to watch *Tsotsi*, a locally made film that won an Oscar in the best foreign film category. During the movie we became aware of people laughing during some of the most painful scenes. People laughed when the gangster character robbed and then killed a train commuter. They laughed when he harassed a paraplegic beggar at the train station. They laughed when he stole the baby. They laughed when flies smothered the baby's face. Afterward, both my son and I were puzzled about why the audience had laughed during these sad moments.

Strangely, a few days later I came across an article in a Johannesburg newspaper. Written by Justice Malala, the article focused on the same question my son and I had struggled with.[7] Movingly, Justice wrote about the violence that had always been part of his growing up in South Africa. Reflecting on the scenes where one would have expected tears, he suggested that the laughter reflected the unhealed groans of a nation that had gone crazy with violence. He wrote, "It has made me realize that all these people were not simply laughing. They have forgotten how to cry."

It is not always easy to listen to the groans of those who have forgotten how to cry!

For Reflection

Read Romans 8:22. Imagine yourself circling the globe, listening carefully to the cries of creation. Where are you drawn to touch down and immerse yourself? Where are you repelled and inclined to flee?

Holy Creator,
Open my heart and soul to the groans of creation. Enable me to pause in this space of vulnerability. Spark my imagination with ways to respond lovingly.
Amen.

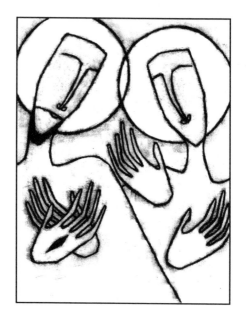

WE GROAN

Not only the creation, but we ourselves, who have the first fruits of the Spirit, groan inwardly.

—Romans 8:23

In verse 23 Paul vividly captures the tension in which the church—the people of God—lives. On the one hand, we experience the joy of the Spirit at work in our lives, the joy of being called God's beloved children, the joy of knowing that our sins have been forgiven, the joy of being bonded together with brothers and sisters in the faith from every tribe and nation and tongue, the joy of knowing that we are living an indestructible life with an eternal future in God's great universe. Through his life, death, and resurrection, Jesus has made all this possible. We are already people of God's new world. We are already people of the new creation. Every time we break the bread and drink the wine, we celebrate this joyful reality.

Yet, on the other hand, we who are part of the church also groan. And we need to listen to and attend to our own groans. In 1978 I had the opportunity of working in a small, ecumenical inner-city congregation in Washington called the Church of the Savior. One day just before I came back to

South Africa, I was having a cup of coffee with the pastor of this remarkable congregation, a man by the name of Gordon Cosby. I asked him a question I sometimes ask people I respect: "If you could say one thing to me, what would it be?" He was quiet for a few moments and then he answered, "When you go back to South Africa and stand up to preach and teach, remember always that each person sits next to their own pool of tears."

I've never forgotten this image. It is an awareness with which I completely live and minister. Each time I speak or teach or gather together in some other way with folk from our local congregation, I am aware that each one of us sits next to a pool of tears. Each one of us carries in our hearts personal wounds as well as the wounds of the nation. Each one of us groans, not only with our own painful longings, but also with the painful longings of that part of the world where we live. As Paul says of us in the church, we also groan.

Let's be sure that we have our ticket. It is as we listen to these groans, present in the midst of our local congregations, that we begin to share in God's great work of healing our world. Dare we believe this? Sometimes in the church we are tempted to look out at the world through the windows of our train as we speed along, willing to criticize what is wrong with the world, analyze its problems, and perhaps even try to solve them; while remaining at a distance. But this is not the way Paul sees the church bringing healing and wholeness. For the apostle, the church does not shout answers at passersby. Rather, the church, as it gathers in local assemblies, shares in the groaning of the world. Right here and now, as we worship, meet in our small groups, and share in our potluck suppers, the pain of our world is present with us, resonating in the agony and anguish of our own hearts.

Paul makes this clear as he describes the parallel groaning of the world and the groaning of the church. Again it has been Tom Wright who has helped me to see the significance of this parallelism.[8] He points out that Paul deliberately uses the same words for the church as he used for the world: *groaning* in verses 22 and 23, and *longing* in verse 19. We in the church are not insulated from the pain of the world. We are not called to rise above the groans of our world into some abstract spiritual sphere of joy and peace and serenity. Instead, we are called to become for the world what Christ was for the world. We are called to become the place and means where the world's pain can be focused and concentrated and shared and even healed. This is how we share in the sufferings of Christ through which the world is made whole.

South Africa is a deeply traumatized country. Literally thousands of people have been violently killed over recent years. For every victim of violence there are five, ten, twenty, maybe a hundred others who are also vicariously affected. Now, these groans are heard whenever the local congregation gathers. The year before last, together with my colleague, we buried eleven victims of violent crime. It is crucial that, in our life together, we listen deeply to each other's stories of pain and grief. In this way we become for each other what Christ was for the world: the place and the means where the pain of our land can be focused and concentrated and held in God's healing presence. And in this way we participate in God's overarching purpose of bringing healing to the world.

For Reflection

Read Romans 8:22–23. Listen for the groans within you. What is the pool of tears beside you, and what is the pain that fills it?

The text also suggests that our groaning arises from our hope. What is the promise for which you yearn, wait, and work?

Son of God,
You know my life intimately. You see those who are connected to my deepest grief and those who are partners in my greatest hope. Hear now–in my sighs–the feelings and longings of my soul.
Amen.

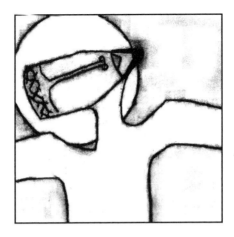

The Spirit Groans

> We do not know how to pray as we ought, but that very Spirit intercedes with sighs too deep for words.
>
> —Romans 8:26

Lastly, we must also listen to the deepest groan of all, the groan of the Spirit. Within the groaning of the world, within the groaning of the church, God groans too. Believing that God groans with us challenges our picture of God. Over the years I have become convinced of the importance of how we understand God. Who is the God we worship? What is our God like? These questions are important because we become like the God we worship. George Bush becomes like the God he worships. Osama bin Laden becomes like the God he worships. Nelson Mandela becomes like the God he worships. Our picture of God has a way of rubbing off on us, shaping the way we see the world, the way we relate to those who suffer, the way we respond to our enemies. Perhaps this is why theologian William Temple once observed that if folks work with a wrong view of God, the more religious they become, the worse it will get and it would be better for them to be atheists.[9]

Paul introduces us to the God who groans. Often we are tempted to think of God as distant, far away, uninvolved in the mess of our world. Bette Midler sings, "God is watching us from a distance."[10] It is a nice song perhaps, but terrible theology! Jesus, who is the image of our invisible God, gives us a different picture. Jesus weeping with Mary and Martha at the grave of Lazarus reminds us that God shares our grief. When Jesus cries out, "My God, my God, why have you forsaken me?" he reminds us that God enters into our places of God-forsakenness and desolation. Even beyond crucifixion, in his transformed resurrection body, Jesus continues to bear the scars. We worship the God who grieves, who weeps, who suffers, and who groans with us and for all the world. When we listen to these groans of God, we become a different kind of church, a different kind of Christ-follower. Wonderfully, we become part of the church that longs to relieve God's suffering in God's people. In Bonhoeffer's striking phrase, we begin to "stand by God in [God's] hour of grieving."[11]

Another aspect I want to highlight is that the groan of the Spirit is the groan of intercession. Go back to verse 26, "that very Spirit intercedes with sighs too deep for words."

Often when we open ourselves to the groans of the world, we come to the end of words. We do not even know how to pray. But the good news is that, in our weakness, the Spirit of God takes the prayer of Jesus and prays it in our own depths. It is the prayer for the coming of God's kingdom, a prayer for God's will to be done, a prayer for heaven to come to earth, a prayer that cares for the groans around us, a prayer for the mending of our broken world.

There is a prayer meeting going on in our hearts 24/7. We are never prayerless! The Spirit is doing the praying that we cannot do. God the Spirit, who shares in the groaning of creation and in our own groaning, is calling out to God the Creator, praying the prayer that resonates in Jesus' own heart for the whole world. There is always a deeply trinitarian shape to Christian prayer.

Do we have the ticket? Will we listen to the groaning of the Spirit who intercedes for us right here, right now? We do not need to get too mystical about this. We are not clueless about what the Spirit may be praying. We know that the Spirit does not talk on the Spirit's own authority. Rather, the Spirit takes the prayer of Jesus and prays it deep within us. It is a prayer for the coming together of all things in Christ.

There was a certain monk who was to an extraordinary degree a man of prayer, someone absolutely carried away by prayer, which was his constant occupation. He was asked once how he had reached that state. He replied that he found it hard to explain. "Looking back," he said, "my impression is that for many, many years I was carrying prayer within my heart, but did not know it at the time. It was like a spring, but one covered by a stone. Then at a certain moment Jesus took the stone away. At that, the spring began to flow and has been flowing ever since."[12]

Will we ask Jesus today to take the stones away from our hearts, so that the prayer which lies there like a hidden spring may begin to overflow throughout our lives and our congregations and our ministries and throughout God's world?

For Reflection

Read Romans 8:26–27. Pause to listen to the groaning of the Spirit, interceding for creation and for us with "sighs too deep for words." To what people or place does the Spirit take you and invite you to open your heart? How is the Spirit calling you to "stand with God"?

Holy Spirit,
Reveal to me those persons with whom you grieve and the places where you groan. Prompt me to stand with them. Give me the courage to go to those places of pain.
Amen.

RESPONDING TO THE GROANS

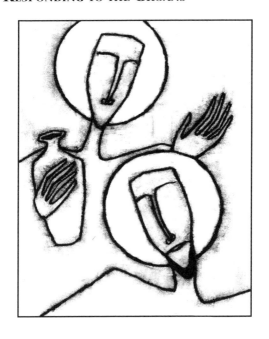

Once we listen to the groans, we will want to respond, desiring to participate in some practical way in God's dream for a healed world. But where do we begin? Obviously, we cannot reach out to all the groans in our midst. We cannot call on all the home-bound elderly; care for all the destitute; visit all the sick, bereaved, and dying. We cannot minister to all those with AIDS, empower all the homeless, educate all the illiterate, visit all the prisoners. But we can ask God, "Which groan has my name written on it?" This is what all the great Christ-followers have done—people like Dorothy Day, Jean Vanier, Mother Teresa, Desmond Tutu, and others—they have sought to discern their own particular call to live out some little piece of God's dream within God's world. We can also do this. Such a question, when accompanied by wrestling prayer and purposeful action, always carries forward God's dream in our midst.

Usually when we discern the part we are called to play in God's dream, we also discover that we cannot do it alone. Then we need to share the concern we feel with those with whom we worship and live out our faith. Others may feel a similar call and decide to join us in a particular ministry. Or we might decide to join an organization or group that is already involved in the area to which we feel drawn. Indeed, one of the most important challenges facing local congregations today is to establish "call groups" who wish to minister to the hungry, call on the sick, follow up with the bereaved, befriend the lonely, and reach out to those who are hurting. Congregations like this have a missional focus that draws them out into God's purposes for the world.

Each one of us has been called to participate in making God's new world real. As we have seen, the whole creation is in labor, longing for this to happen. The church, you and I, are already part of God's new creation. Now we are called to implement this new creation wherever our world groans in pain and hope. We are called to do this through our prayers and actions, through our storytelling and our symbols, through our work and our worship. But before we can do any of these things faithfully, there is one thing we must do. We must make sure that we have our ticket. We must listen to the groans.

For Reflection

Read Romans 8:22–27. Listen for the Spirit that "intercedes for the saints according to the will of God" for all creation. Listen for the part you ("the saints") are called to play in making God's new world real. What is God's prayer for you and for the part you will play in God's dream? What would it mean for you to be an answer to God's prayer?

God of Transformation,
Open my eyes to see the sorrow and hurt that is undeniably part of creation. May my prayers for hope and healing be joined with the deep sighs of the Spirit. And may all the prayers of creation bring about mending and reconciliation and the oneness of creation with the Creator.
Amen.

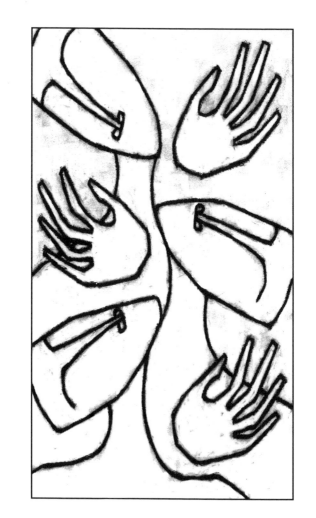

Listening to the Groans
PILGRIMAGE AND RETREAT

Purpose

This retreat gives persons who have read *Listening to the Groans* together an experience of pilgrimage into the suffering, need, and hope in their own communities. It will also provide retreat time to reflect on the shared learnings from the reading, as well as time to process and debrief the pilgrimage itself.

Specific purpose and requests:

- to visit as pilgrims (not missionaries or tourists)
- to be with the people for part of a day (3–4 hours) and hear their stories
- to talk with leaders and caregivers who attend to the suffering
- to share a simple meal
- to do no harm

Possible pilgrimage sites:

- homeless shelter or day shelter for homeless persons
- community center in an impoverished section of town
- church–based programs that care for the poor, homeless, or other groups in need
- domestic violence or teenage runaway shelters
- rehabilitation center for those in recovery from addictions

Advance Preparation

Preparing spiritually.
Listening to the Groans introduces an important aspect of discipleship, inviting prayer and deep listening that open persons to new experiences. Additionally, it will be important for everyone in the group to pray specifically for the pilgrimage and for those who will be encountered in this brief

journey. It will also be helpful to remind participants that while we can plan for many things, we cannot control all factors or ensure particular outcomes of a pilgrimage. A certain spiritual detachment, or freedom from worry about how we will be received, facilitates opening to the movement of the Spirit.

Prepare materials and the meeting space(s).
A variety of tasks will need to be accomplished to make the pilgrimage and retreat a meaningful experience. In order to get these things done, everyone in your group should be assigned to work on some aspect of these tasks: site selection, food, transportation, worship, and meeting facilitation.

Pilgrimage and Retreat

FRIDAY EVENING

6:00   Gather for dinner (potluck or other simple fare)

7:00   Opening worship

- Invite silence for centering/adoration; meditative music optional
- Light the Christ candle and say words to the following effect:

  We are gathered in the living presence of Christ once again. Through the experiences of this retreat, we will have a chance to reflect on where we have come by God's grace and ways we may be changing. Through this evening's retreat time we will prepare ourselves for tomorrow's pilgrimage. Tomorrow we will reflect on our experiences and contemplate ways we might continue our spiritual journeys.

- Sing or play a hymn or song. Suggestion: "Be Thou My Vision" (UMH #451)

- Read a psalm of praise, followed by silence.
- Offer a prayer.

7:15   Sharing insights from the reading
   –What, if any, changes do you sense at work in you as you have read this booklet?
   –What have you identified as anticipation or anxiety related to tomorrow's pilgrimage?
   –When during these recent weeks did you find yourself experiencing a deeper awareness of God's presence?
- Invite group members to share insights. Remind them that the task of those listening is to attend fully to each speaker without fixing, judging, or proselytizing. As the leader, begin the sharing time with your own experiences.

- Conclude by asking the group members

to identify common themes they heard in the sharing time.

8:00   Overview of the pilgrimage site and plans for tomorrow. Make sure everyone knows where to be, what to bring, and what time to gather in the morning.

8:15   Deeper Explorations
Together we have been planning a pilgrimage that will take place tomorrow. It will be a brief encounter with people suffering in our city (county, or region). We might think of the process we are now sharing in four parts: preparation, encounter, reflection, and transformation. As noted before, we can plan, pray, encounter, and even reflect, but none of these things guarantee transformation. Instead, transformation is a gift that we hope for and sometimes see only in hindsight.

As part of our preparation for tomorrow's pilgrimage, let's explore the wisdom of a New Testament story to see what it tells us about preparation, encounter, reflection, and transformation.

- Read Luke 24:13–35 slowly for the group. Ask people to listen for instances of preparation, encounter, reflection, and transformation as the story is read. Then work together as a group to list on the board or newsprint what you heard related to each phase of this process of pilgrimage. The following ideas may stimulate discussion if needed.

  –*Preparation*: These disciples had been with Jesus for some time; they knew from firsthand experience about his teaching, his healing, and all the events of recent days including his trial and crucifixion; they had been preparing for this encounter for a long time, although they may not have realized it fully until looking back.

–*Encounter*: The two disciples had a profound encounter with pain and hope over just the past week. Make a list of their personal groans and the groans of others they may have heard; describe the hope they held; describe their encounter with the stranger on the road in the midst of their deep suffering and grief.

–*Reflection*: They recounted to the stranger what they had seen and heard; they reflected with the stranger as he told them biblical stories and shed new light on them; the disciples reflected with each other; they broke bread together and in that act their eyes were opened; they noticed their feelings (burning hearts) when they looked back at the walk with the stranger on the Emmaus road.

–*Transformation*: Note what seemed to be the key to the disciples' transformation: encountering and recognizing the living Christ. Also note what happened when they experienced a change of feeling, attitude, and understanding: they got up and ran back to the city–the place of pain and suffering–with renewed hope, and there they encountered the risen Christ again.

• Ask the following:

What can we learn from this New Testament story for our pilgrimage tomorrow?

Spend a few moments drawing connections to the anticipated pilgrimage. Use the following questions to guide discussion:

–How have our lives been preparing us for tomorrow?

–How might our encounters with strangers turn out to be encounters with Christ?

–How can we attend deeply to the situation and the people we will meet?

• Invite a time of intercessory prayer for the group, individuals in the group, the people you will meet tomorrow, and the complex systems of pain and suffering that make this pilgrimage important.

9:00   Evening prayers
• Select a song, scripture, prayer, and blessing; or use an evening prayer service from your tradition.

9:15   Sending forth

SATURDAY MORNING
8:00   Morning prayers

(coffee, tea, or juice may be offered)
- Silence, scripture, prayer, song, blessing; or use a morning prayer service from your tradition

8:30   Travel to the pilgrimage site

9:00   Meet with clients or residents and caregivers at the site
(Fill in this part of the schedule with the details of your particular pilgrimage.)

12:00   Shared lunch at the pilgrimage site

1:00   Return to the retreat site

1:30   Individual reflection and journaling time
- When the group returns to the retreat site, invite members to spend time in personal reflection and writing in their journals. Ask them to record what they

noticed as they attended to the place, the people, and the circumstances of the pilgrimage. Ask them also to record what they noticed about their own reactions, feelings, and inner experiences while they were at the site. And finally, ask them to write down what they noticed about God's presence, promptings, or nudges while they were there. In other words, ask them to listen deeply to the situation and the people, to themselves, and to God's Spirit.

2:15   Group reflection

- Call participants back to the whole group and debrief your experiences together.
- Light the Christ candle and offer a prayer for open hearts and minds.
- Set a context for reflection.

Having been on many pilgrimages, the author observes that when we open our eyes and our lives to suffering persons, three things emerge: "The Spirit of God opens blind eyes, uncovers inner poverty, [and] reveals hidden riches."[13]

As you reflect together, use the following two categories written on newsprint or a dry-erase board:

"Outer pain, poverty, suffering"

"Inner pain, poverty, suffering"

- Begin by naming what participants observed as the outer pain, poverty, and suffering in the situation. List them on the board. How were their eyes opened? How are they seeing the world differently? Then move to what these observations stirred in their own souls. What inner pain, poverty of spirit, or personal suffering did this experience reveal?

- Say:

  We have focused on the part of this pilgrimage that evoked pain and suffering, and we have attended to the ways we also share in that pain and suffering as part of God's creation. Now we want to spend time noticing what hidden riches were uncovered in this experience.

Write the following two categories on newsprint or the board:

"Hidden riches, joy, hope of others"

"Hidden riches, joy, hope in us"

- Ask participants to name the riches of hope and joy that they witnessed at the pilgrimage site. Ask them what inner joy or hope it stirred in their own being. What new resources in their lives may have been called forth by this experience? What encouragement, healing, or transformation does this hope suggest?

• Say in your own words:

Pilgrimage does not have to be a one–time, special event. The way of the pilgrim can be the daily way of life for a Christ–follower. Consider for a few moments what such a commitment to pilgrimage might mean for your life.

Allow a time of silent reflection.

• Close the group reflection time with a period of prayer in which participants can pray aloud as the Spirit leads.

Break (10 minutes)

3:00   Closing Communion or Love Feast
   • Read scripture (Luke 24:28–35).
   • Share in moment of silent reflection.
   • Use the communion liturgy from your tradition. A Love Feast service is

found in *The United Methodist Book of Worship* (pages 581–84[14] or search online at http://www.gbod.org/worship). Offer a blessing or the words of institution for the bread and cup.

- Share in Holy Communion by passing the elements around the circle. The first person should hold the plate and cup while the second person tears off bread, dips it in the cup, and eats. This way the group is sharing a common cup, symbolizing shared suffering and hope.
- Sing or say a benediction.

3:30   Sending forth

Notes

1. Dietrich Bonhoeffer, *Life Together*, trans. John W. Doberstein (San Francisco: HarperSan-Francisco, 1954), 97–98.

2. Tom Wright, *The Crown and the Fire: Meditations on the Cross and the Life of the Spirit* (London: SPCK Publishing, 1992), 68.

3. "I Have Decided to Follow Jesus," *The Baptist Hymnal* (Nashville, Tenn.: Convention Press, 1991), no. 305.

4. "Turn Your Eyes upon Jesus," lyrics by Helen H. Lemmel, *The United Methodist Hymnal* (Nashville, Tenn.: The United Methodist Publishing House, 1989), no. 349.

5. Hans Küng, *On Being a Christian*, trans. Edward Quinn (London: William Collins, 1977), 231.

6. See Richard Lischer, *The End of Words: The Language of Reconciliation in a Culture of Violence* (Grand Rapids, Mich.: William B. Eerdmans Publishing Company, 2005).

7. Justice Malala, "Laughter and Forgetting," *Sunday Times* (April 2, 2006).

8. See Wright, *The Crown and the Fire*, 72–74.

9. Kenneth Leech, *Spirituality and Pastoral Care* (London: SPCK Publishing, 1986), 50.

10. "From a Distance," lyrics by Julie Gold, *Bette Midler: Greatest Hits—Experience the Divine* (Atlantic/Wea, 1993).

11. Dietrich Bonhoeffer, *Letters and Papers from Prison*, ed. E. Bethge (New York: Macmillan, 1953), 349.

12. Andre Louf, *Teach Us to Pray: Learning a Little about Prayer*, trans. H. Hoskyns (London: Darton, Longman & Todd, 1991).

13. Trevor Hudson, *A Mile in My Shoes* (Nashville, Tenn.: Upper Room Books, 2005), 43.

14. "The Love Feast," *The United Methodist Book of Worship* (Nashville, Tenn.: The United Methodist Publishing House, 1992), 581–84.

About the Authors

Trevor Hudson is married to Debbie, and together they are the parents of Joni and Mark. He has been in the Methodist ministry in South Africa for over thirty years, spending most of this time in and around Johannesburg. Presently, he is part of the pastoral team at Northfield Methodist Church in Benoni, where he preaches and teaches on a weekly basis. Trevor travels internationally and leads conferences, retreats, and workshops in diverse settings.

Stephen D. Bryant is editor and publisher of Upper Room Ministries. His vision of small groups as important settings for spiritual formation and his experience in the contemplative life as well as local churches provided the inspiration for the Companions in Christ series.

About the Artist

Jan L. Richardson serves as director of The Wellspring Studio, LLC, a ministry that incorporates her vocation as an artist, writer, spiritual director, and ordained minister in the United Methodist Church. She is Visiting Artist at First United Methodist Church of Winter Park, Florida; travels widely as a retreat and workshop leader; and is a faculty member of the Grünewald Guild in Leavenworth, Washington. Jan's books include *Sacred Journeys*, *Night Visions*, and *In Wisdom's Path*. Visit Jan's Web site at www.janrichardson.com.